The Frugal English Paleo Cook:
Budget Recipes For Gluten-Free/Paleo Dishes Suited For British Tastes

By Michelle Newbold

Published by Budding Books

Copyright Notice

P is for … Paleo!

Introduction:

For some years now there has been the belief that following a diet similar to that eaten by man during the Palaeolithic era would improve a person's health.

Evolution is a very slow process, and the human body is still engineered to survive on a diet made up of chiefly fats and protein, with only small amounts of naturally occurring carbohydrates.

With the agricultural revolution, and domestication of animals roughly 10,000 years ago, humans started consuming large amounts of dairy products, beans, cereals, alcohol and salt.

These dietary changes have been blamed for many of the so-called "diseases of civilization" and other chronic illnesses that are found today, such as obesity, cardiovascular disease, high blood pressure, type 2 diabetes, osteoporosis, autoimmune diseases, colorectal cancer, myopia, acne, depression, and diseases related to vitamin and mineral deficiencies.

For quite a few years doctors have recommended a gluten-free diet for patients coming to them suffering from colitis, Crohn's disease, irritable bowel syndrome and indigestion. Illnesses that were not really heard of before the agricultural revolution some 10,000 years ago before the introduction of grains and legumes into the human diet.

Since the Palaeolithic diet does not include cereal grains, it is naturally gluten-free. The paleo diet also does not include milk, so is also casein-free. Casein is a protein found in milk and dairy products, which may affect glucose tolerance in humans.

Since the end of the 1990s, a number of medical doctors and nutritionists have championed a return to a Palaeolithic diet approach, and a number of them have written books and created websites on the subject.

A true Palaeolithic diet is made up of foods that can be hunted and fished, such as fish, meat and poultry, or can be gathered or picked, such as eggs, fruit, nuts, seeds and vegetables.

Our modern lifestyles obviously do not allow us to hunt or gather our food anymore, so we have to adapt our diet to consume commonly available foods found in our local shops and supermarkets.

With the majority of Paleo/Caveman recipe books coming from American authors, this collection of recipes is more suited to people in the UK or who have more British tastes, and uses foods that are easily picked up at local supermarkets and shops.

This book is also aimed at people who are looking for budget recipes, and don't want to spend too much time preparing complicated dishes using hard to find ingredients.

I hope you enjoy them….

Contents:

Dishes using beef mince as a base.

Beef mince is used the world over as a cheap and quick-cooking form of beef. Some of its most well known uses are in beef burgers, sausages and cottage pie. It is a main ingredient in meatloaf, meatballs and tacos.

The Scottish dish mince and tatties uses beef mince along with mashed potatoes. But it's not just people in the UK who use a lot of mince, in Italy it is used in meat sauces for lasagne and spaghetti Bolognese.

Raw lean ground beef is used to make steak tartare, a delicious French dish.
Picadillo is the Spanish term for ground beef, and is a well known ingredient in several Latin American cuisines.

When buying beef mince try to buy good quality fresh mince rather than the cheap and nasty frozen stuff that is a mixture of beef and pork mince. Using the nasty stuff will result in a tasteless mush swimming in greasy fat that will ruin the flavour and consistency of any dish you go on to use it in.

Mince freezes very well, so if you see good quality packs at reduced prices in the supermarket, buy them up and freeze them down for future use.

The following recipes are based on beef mince as either the main ingredient, or an important part of it. You could substitute beef mince for pork, chicken or turkey mince, but the resulting flavour would not compare to using good quality beef mince.

Home Made Beef Burgers

serves 4-6
1kg/2¼lb lean minced beef
1 large onion, grated
3 tbsp fresh parsley and thyme
Salt and pepper, to taste

Preheat the grill to hot.
Place all the ingredients in a large bowl and mix together with your hands.
With wet hands, shape the meat into flattish round burger shapes of an equal depth to ensure even cooking.
Cook under the grill for approximately 5 minutes on each side - the burgers should be brown in the middle as well as on the outside.

Super Hot Chilli Beefburgers

Serves 8
900g (2 lb) lean minced beef
2 cloves garlic, crushed
2 green chillies, seeded and minced
2 hot chilli peppers of your choice, deseeded and
finely chopped
1 teaspoon cayenne pepper
handful chopped fresh coriander
1 teaspoon ground cumin

Preheat grill to a high heat.
In a large mixing bowl, combine all the
ingredients with your hands. Form into burger
shaped patties.
Cook burgers for about 5 minutes per side, or
until done right through.

Spicy Burgers

Serves 4
1 tsp ground coriander
1 tsp ground cumin
Pinch of chilli flakes
Pinch of ground ginger
2 clove garlic, crushed
1 onion, finely chopped
400g/14 oz lean minced beef
Salt and freshly ground black pepper
2tbsp olive oil

Preheat the oven to 200C/400F/Gas 6.
To make the burgers: Place the ground spices and
chilli into a bowl and add the garlic, onion and
minced beef. Mix together well with your hands,
seasoning with salt and freshly ground black
pepper. Shape the mince mixture into flat burger
shapes.
Heat the olive oil in a frying pan over a medium
heat. Add the two patties and fry for two minutes
on each side just to colour them. Transfer the
burgers to a baking sheet and place into the oven
to bake for 8-10 minutes, or until completely
cooked through.

Spicy Beef Koftas

for 4 koftas
175g/6oz lean minced beef
¼ tsp ground turmeric powder
1 garlic clove, peeled
¼ tsp dried chilli flakes
Pinch of salt
2 tsp dried oregano
2 tsp ground coriander seeds
Olive oil, for frying

1 small bunch of fresh parsley leaves
2 tbsp olive oil
Salt and freshly ground black pepper

For the koftas, soak five wooden skewers in a
bowl of water for ten minutes to prevent the
sticks from burning during cooking.
Place all of the kofta ingredients except the olive
oil into a food processor and blend until smooth.
Use your hands to divide the mixture into five
equal portions and squeeze the mixture around
the top half of the skewers.
Heat the olive oil in a large frying pan over a
high heat. Fry the koftas on both sides for about
5-6 minutes until cooked through.

For the herb salad, mix the parsley leaves with
the olive oil and seasoning in a bowl.

To serve, place the herb salad in the middle of a plate and arrange the koftas on top.

Meatballs With Chilli and Cumin In Tomato Salsa

Serves 2
For the meatballs
1 small onion, finely chopped
2 garlic clove, finely chopped
300g lean minced beef
1 tsp cumin seeds
1 tsp freshly grated nutmeg
1 tsp chilli flakes
Salt and freshly ground black pepper
2 tbsp chopped fresh mint
3 tbsp olive oil

For the tomato salsa
2 tbsp olive oil
100g/3½oz cherry tomatoes, chopped
½ red onion, finely chopped
½ red pepper, finely chopped
small handful fresh mint, chopped
A squeeze of fresh lemon juice
A pinch dried chilli flakes
Salt and black pepper

Make the salsa first so it has time for the flavours to develop while the meatballs are cooking.
For the salsa, place the olive oil, chopped tomatoes, onion, pepper, mint, lemon juice and chilli flakes into a small mixing bowl, season well with salt and black pepper.

16

Place all the meatball ingredients except for the olive oil in a large mixing bowl and mix well using your hands. Pinch out walnut-sized pieces of the mixture and roll into balls. Heat the oil in a frying pan and fry the meatballs for 5-6 minutes, or until coloured on all sides and completely cooked through. Check one for doneness. Once cooked through, remove the meatballs from the pan and arrange onto warm plates. Top with some of the tomato salsa, and serve with some fresh baby spinach leaves.

Meatball Curry

Serves 4
450g/1lb lean minced beef
1 tsp crushed garlic
1 large onion, finely chopped
½ tsp black pepper
1 tsp garam masala spice
1 free-range egg
1 tsp olive oil
1 tsp ground cumin
1 tsp finely chopped root ginger
1 x 400g/14oz tin chopped tomatoes
1 tsp tomato purée
½ tsp ground turmeric

Mix the beef, garlic, half of the onion, pepper,
garam masala and egg together in a mixing bowl.
Use your hands to shape the mixture into 24 even
sized meatballs.
Preheat the grill to hot.
Line the bottom of a grill tray with foil to make
the grill easier to clean afterwards, and place the
meatballs under the grill. Grill the meatballs
under a medium heat for about 10 to 15 minutes,
turning occasionally until cooked through.
Heat the olive oil in a large frying pan, and add
the rest of the onion and cumin powder. Cook for
5 minutes until softened, then stir in the ginger.
Add the tin of chopped tomatoes, tomato purée
and turmeric, mix well and cook for 10 to 15

minutes until the sauce has reduced a little and thickened.
Add back in the cooked meatballs, reduce the heat and simmer for 20 minutes. If the sauce looks like its going a bit dry, add a little water.

Mince With Butternut Mash

Serves 2
50g/2oz lard
1 small onion, finely chopped
A pinch of ground coriander
A pinch of ground cumin
A pinch of chilli flakes
A pinch ground ginger
500g/18oz lean minced beef
2 tbsp tomato purée
100ml/4fl oz hot gluten free beef stock
1 Butternut squash, peeled and seeds removed

To make the mince, melt the lard in a large
saucepan, over a medium heat. Add the onion
and cook for 2-3 minutes until softened and
opaque.
Add the spices and stir well to combine.
Add the mince, and cook until it has browned and
there are no pink bits left.
Add the tomato purée, hot beef stock and cook
for a few minutes or until the sauce has reduced a
little, and is slightly thickened.

To make the butternut mash, place the butternut
squash into a pan of boiling water and boil for 10
minutes, or until soft, then mash. Season with salt
and black pepper, and serve with the mince.

Paleo Beef Tacos

Serves 6
500g lean beef mince
1 onion, chopped
1 green pepper, chopped
1 garlic clove, crushed
1/2 teaspoon hot paprika
1/4 teaspoon ground cumin
1/4 teaspoon dried red chilli flakes
6 tablespoons tomato puree
Olive oil or lard for frying
Salt and black pepper to taste
1 iceberg lettuce,
2 tomatoes, finely chopped
1 avocado, diced

Fry the beef mince in a little olive oil or lard in a frying pan until brown and crumbly, stirring occasionally and breaking it up with a wooden spoon so there are no lumps.
Add the onion, green pepper and garlic; fry, stirring occasionally, until softened. Stir in the herbs and spices; season to taste with salt and black pepper. Add the tomato puree and mix well. Cover and cook gently for about 10 to 12 minutes, stirring occasionally.
Once cooked through, place a little of the mixture in an iceberg lettuce leaf, top with the tomato and avocado, roll up and enjoy.

Love It Or Hate It Marmite Mince

(Beware people with allergies: Marmite is made with brewers yeast, so anyone with a yeast allergy should steer clear of this one)

Serves 4
1 tablespoon of clarified butter or lard
2 small onions - diced
450g/1 lb lean beef mince
2 dessertspoons of marmite
1 250g punnet of mushrooms, cleaned and sliced
1 teaspoon paprika
2 gluten free beef stock cubes, melted in 250ml (8 fl oz) of hot water

Melt the butter or lard in a wok over medium heat. Add the onions, and fry until soft.
Stir in the beef mince and fry until browned and there are no pink bits left.
Scrape the beef and onion out to the edges of the pan, leaving a pool of fat in the centre. Stir the marmite into the fat, and mix well. Combine with mince and onions.
Stir in the paprika, and the beef stock. Bring everything back to the boil, and once everything is heated through it is ready to serve.

Serve with mashed Swede or turnip, or vegetables of your choice.

Paleo Spaghetti Mince

Serves 6
1 dessertspoon olive oil
1 garlic clove, crushed
1 onion, finely chopped
500g lean beef mince
2 carrots, finely chopped
1 tablespoon tomato puree
1 400g tin chopped tomatoes
250ml gluten free beef stock
1/2 tsp salt
1/4 tsp black pepper
1/4 tsp mixed dried herbs

For the spaghetti:
Courgettes, washed and cut into slivers using a vegetable peeler

Heat the oil in a large saucepan and brown the garlic, onions and mince until there are no pink bits left.
Add the carrots and celery and cook until the vegetables are tender.
Stir in the puree, stock, tomatoes and herbs.
Cover and simmer for 40 minutes.

While the mince is cooking, wash the courgettes and using a vegetable peeler, slice long strips of courgette to resemble the ribbon pasta you used to eat.

Boil the courgette strips lightly in a little salted water for 5 minutes, drain and divide onto plates, serve with a generous portion of beef mince sauce spooned over the top.

Cottage Pie

Serves 4
1 tablespoon olive oil
1 large onion, chopped
1 clove garlic, crushed
2 medium carrots, chopped
500g lean beef mince
1 400g tin chopped tomatoes
2 tablespoons tomato purée
300ml gluten free beef stock
1 teaspoon dried mixed herbs
A dash of Worcestershire sauce
Salt and black pepper to taste
For the topping:
1kg pumpkin flesh peeled and diced (or another
squash if pumpkin is unavailable)
2 teaspoons Dijon mustard
75g clarified butter or Ghee (or use olive oil if
you don't want to use butter)

Preheat the oven to 190 C / Gas mark 5.
Heat the oil in a large frying pan over medium
high heat. Add the onion, garlic and carrot and
cook over a medium heat until the vegetables are
soft. Add the mince and cook until brown and no
pink bits remain.
3. Add the tinned tomatoes, purée, beef stock,
mixed herbs and Worcestershire sauce. Season to
taste with salt and pepper. Cover and simmer
gently for 30 minutes.

While the mince is simmering, boil the pumpkin or squash in lightly salted water until soft. Drain and mash with the mustard and butter. Season with salt and pepper to taste. Add a handful of your favourite chopped herbs for a bit of extra colour if you like.

5. Spoon the mince mixture into a casserole dish. Top with the mashed pumpkin, drizzle the top with a little olive oil and bake for 30 minutes until golden brown all over.

Beef And Spinach Chilli

Serves 6
450g lean beef mince
1 large onion, chopped
1 400g tin chopped tomatoes
420g tomato passata (sieved tomatoes)
400g frozen spinach, thawed
1 teaspoon chilli powder
1 teaspoon ground cumin
1/2 teaspoon ground cayenne pepper
1 teaspoon minced garlic

In a large saucepan over medium-high heat, cook
the beef and onion until the mince has browned
through. Stir in the tinned tomatoes, passata,
spinach, chilli powder, cumin, cayenne and
garlic. Cover, reduce heat and simmer slowly for
20 minutes.

Traditional Meatloaf

Serves 8
2 large onions, finely chopped
2 large celery sticks, finely chopped
1 large red pepper, deseeded and finely chopped
3 garlic cloves, crushed
900g/2lb lean minced beef
1 large egg
Black pepper to taste
1 400g tin chopped tomatoes
2 tbsp tomato paste

Preheat the oven to 180°C (350°F, gas mark 4).
Grease a large loaf tin or baking dish with a little
olive oil. Sauté the onions, celery, green pepper
and garlic in a little oil for about 5 minutes or
until soft. Transfer the vegetables to a large
mixing bowl. Add the beef mince, egg and black
pepper to the vegetables and mix everything
together well. Combine the tinned tomatoes with
the tomato puree in another bowl. Add half of the
tomato mix to the meat mixture, and mix this in
well to combine.
Spoon the meat mixture into the loaf tin or
baking dish, press down and smooth the surface.
Pour the remaining tomato mixture over the top.
Bake the meatloaf for about 1¼ hours or until
completely cooked through. Leave to stand for 10
minutes before slicing.

Traditional meatloaf. Probably my favourite way to use minced beef.

Mince and Vegetable Soup

Serves 8
450g carrots, cut into chunks
300g fresh mushrooms, sliced
1/2 Savoy cabbage, sliced
425g peeled and cubed butternut squash
2 400g tins chopped tomatoes
120ml gluten free vegetable stock
450g lean minced beef
A pinch of chilli powder
A pinch of paprika
A pinch of cumin
½ teaspoon oregano
1/2 teaspoon salt
½ teaspoon of black pepper
1 clove garlic, crushed

Place the carrots in a large, heavy saucepan, then add the mushrooms, Savoy cabbage, butternut squash, tomatoes and vegetable stock on top. Cover and bring to the boil over medium-high heat.
While the soup is coming to the boil, heat a large frying pan over medium-high heat and fry the mince with the crushed garlic, spices, salt and pepper. Cook and stir until the beef is evenly browned. Drain the mince and add to the soup, reduce heat to medium, and simmering for about 1 hour. Season again if needed and serve.

Paprika Mince

Serves 4
1 large onion, cut into slices
1 clove garlic, crushed
1 tablespoon olive oil
450g/1 lb lean minced beef
1 tablespoon paprika
1 tablespoon tomato puree
4 tomatoes, peeled and quartered
Salt and black pepper to taste
150ml/6 fl oz gluten free beef stock

Fry the onion and garlic in the olive oil until
lightly browned.
Stir in the mince and cook until it has browned
through and no pink bits remain.
Add the paprika, tomato paste, tomatoes, and
stock. Bring to the boil, turn down to medium-
low heat and leave to simmer for 30 mins,
stirring occasionally. Season with salt and black
pepper to taste and serve.

Easy Beef and Vegetable Patties

500g lean beef mince
1/2 courgette, grated
2 carrots, grated
2 tablespoons cayenne pepper, or less if you
prefer
Salt and black pepper to taste
1 large egg
1 tablespoon olive oil

Mix together all ingredients except the oil.
Use your hands to roll into golf ball-sized rounds
and flatten to 1cm thick.
Refrigerate for one hour after all the ingredients
are mixed for the flavour to really come out.
Fry in the olive oil in a large pan at medium heat
until cooked through.

I sometimes vary this recipe by using up whatever vegetables or herbs I have left in the fridge. These are made with parsley and spring onions.

Slow Cooker Mince Stew

Serves 4
1 tablespoon olive oil
1 onion, chopped
2 cloves garlic, crushed
600g lean minced beef
125ml gluten free beef stock
2 tablespoons tomato puree
1 tablespoon oregano
salt and pepper

Heat the olive oil in a frying pan. Brown the onion and the garlic for 5-10 minutes over low heat, then place in the slow cooker.
Turn up the heat and brown the mince in the frying pan until no trace of pink is left.
Add the stock, tomato puree, oregano, salt and pepper, mix well and transfer to the slow cooker.
Cook on High for 2 hours then turn down to Low for 2 more hours.

Minced Beef Stir Fry

Serves 2
Olive oil for frying
1 large onion, sliced
250g lean beef mince
Salt and pepper
1 pinch of ground coriander
1 pinch of ground cumin
1 heaped teaspoon Chinese five spice powder
1/2 teaspoon ginger paste
1/2 Savoy cabbage, finely shredded

Heat 2 tablespoons of olive oil in a wok or deep frying pan on medium heat and add the onion. Fry for about 5 minutes until slightly softened then add the beef mince. Stir well to break up any lumps and brown until there is no pink left. Add the coriander, cumin, five spice, ginger, salt and pepper. Cook for a few minutes more, turn the heat to low and simmer for 10 minutes stirring occasionally.
While the mince is cooking, heat a little oil then add the cabbage. Add 100ml water, and stir well. Cover and cook on a low heat for 8 to 10 minutes. Drain the cabbage and add to the meat. Stir well to combine and cook for another 5 minutes. Serve.

Mince, Cabbage and Carrot Stir Fry

Serves: 4
2 tablespoons olive oil
4 cloves garlic, chopped
225g lean minced beef
1/2 small green cabbage, shredded
1 red pepper, cut into strips
1 carrot, peeled and sliced into ribbons
120ml water
1 tablespoon Chinese five spice powder
1 teaspoon black pepper

Heat a wok or large frying pan over medium-high heat, and add oil. Sauté garlic for about 5 seconds, then add the minced beef. Stir-fry until beef is evenly brown. Stir in cabbage, carrots and pepper, and cook until all the vegetables are tender, and beef is fully cooked through. Stir in the Chinese five spice powder and water. Season with pepper. Heat everything through and cook for another 5 minutes, then serve.

Sloppy Joes

Serves 8
675g minced beef
1 onion, chopped
1 red pepper, chopped
175g tomato puree
250ml water
3 cloves garlic, minced
1 tablespoon chilli powder
1 teaspoon paprika
1 teaspoon ground cumin
3 tablespoons runny honey
1 teaspoon dried oregano
1/2 teaspoon salt
1/2 teaspoon ground black pepper

In a large frying pan over medium-high heat, sauté the minced beef for 5 minutes until brown. Add the onion and red pepper; sauté for 5 more minutes, or until onion is cooked through and opaque. Drain off the excess fat.
Mix in tomato puree and water, stirring until puree is dissolved. Stir in garlic, chilli powder, paprika, cumin, honey, oregano, salt and pepper. Continue to cook for 5 to 10 minutes, then serve.

Beef With Mushroom And Onion

Serves 4
300g minced beef
Pinch salt
Pinch black pepper
1 tablespoon olive oil
1 large onion, sliced
1 teaspoon chopped garlic
150g fresh mushrooms, sliced
3 tablespoons tomato puree
5 tablespoons tomato passata or sieved tomatoes
5 tablespoons boiling water
1 tablespoon Worcestershire sauce
1 gluten free chicken stock cube

Fry the beef mince in the hot oil until brown.
When browned, add chopped garlic and onion
slices. When onion has cooked, add the
mushrooms and continue to cook over gentle
heat.
In a separate bowl, mix together tomato puree,
passata, boiling water, Worcestershire sauce, and
chicken stock cube. Stir well to dissolve stock
cube.
Pour the mixture over the beef and onions, cover
and allow to come to the boil. Simmer for 2 to 3
minutes then serve.

Pork And Beef Meatballs

Serves 2
1 teaspoon dried tarragon
200g lean steak mince
200g pork mince
1 large egg
salt and pepper to taste
1 tablespoon redcurrant jelly
1 pinch ground allspice
1 pinch ground nutmeg
1 onion, very finely diced
1 teaspoon Dijon or grainy mustard
olive oil for pan frying

Mix all other ingredients, except for the oil, and
using your hands mix well and then shape into
small meatballs. Place onto a plate, cover and
chill to let the flavours develop.
Heat some olive oil in a frying pan over medium
heat and pan fry until the meatballs are browned
all over and cooked through for about 15
minutes.
Drain on kitchen paper for a minute before
serving on warmed plates.

Mince Stuffed Peppers

Serves 4
360g bagged frozen mixed veg
1 tablespoon olive oil
1 large onion, chopped
500g lean mince or steak mince
1 gluten free beef stock cube
2 pinches salt
2 pinches black pepper
1 pinch mixed herbs
4 peppers (yellow, orange or red are sweetest)

Add the 360g of veg to a saucepan of boiling water with a pinch of salt (boil for 5 minutes). Drain.
Add the olive oil to a pan over medium high heat. Add the onion and cook for 5 minutes. Add the mince and cook till browned and no pink bits are left.
Crumble in the beef stock cube with the black pepper, a pinch of salt and the mixed herbs.
Mix the cooked vegetables and cooked mince together.
Cut the tops off the peppers and hollow them out removing the seeds.
Spoon the mince and vegetable mixture into the peppers making sure they are completely filled.
Put the tops of the peppers back on.

Stand them in a baking dish and place in a 180 C
/ Gas 4 oven and bake until the peppers start to
look like the edges are going brown.

Paleo Corned Beef Hash

OK so not quite a recipe using mined beef, but when you are trying to make ends meet, a tin of corned beef is a handy standby to keep in your kitchen cupboard.

Serves 4
1 Large cauliflower
1 200g tin of corned beef, cut into bite sized chunks
1 large onion, chopped
1/2 pint gluten free beef stock

In a large deep pan, over medium heat, combine the cauliflower, corned beef, onion and stock.
2. Cover and simmer until the cauliflower is cooked, and the liquid almost boiled away. Serve hot in deep bowls.

Using Cheaper Cuts Of Poultry

In an ideal world I would be telling you to only buy the best free-range, organic chickens you can afford, but to most people living on a budget, it is unrealistic to expect you to do this all the time.

However, if you can plan your shopping trips to within the last hour before your supermarket closes, you can often pick up fresh chickens that have been reduced in price to clear.

Admittedly this is a bit harder to do with 24-hour supermarkets, but you may be lucky with smaller supermarkets that have shorter opening hours, or those that don't open overnight.

The same tactic can apply to local farmers markets. Try to time your visits to when the market is winding down, and you will find a lot of food stall holders will drop the price of their produce to get rid of it rather than face having to pack it up and transport it home again.

I'm luck enough to live in a town with a farmers market every Saturday. If you go between 2pm and 3pm there are so many bargains to be had that I often come home with a large bag of discounted fruit and vegetables, along with a nice bit of locally produced meat for a Sunday roast at a bargain price.

Whether you use free-range chickens or not, cooking a whole chicken means you can make a few meals from it. Obviously you can roast the chicken then slice off the breasts and remove the legs for your Sunday roast. Then pick the carcass to strip it of the meat that can go on to be used in other dishes.

But don't throw away the bones! Use the bones to make homemade chicken stock. This makes sense if you are trying to avoid using shop bought stock cubes that often contain gluten and corn starch.

If you come across some bargain chickens on your shopping trips, then remember they can be frozen and used later. Usually it is wise to use your frozen chickens within three months of freezing, after this time the quality of the meat starts to degrade.

Defrost chicken as slowly as possible in the fridge - quick thawing increases the risk of food poisoning. Remove any giblets to allow the thawing to start from inside the cavity. It will probably take around two days for a medium-sized bird to defrost completely.

You will often find that bagged frozen chicken portions are quite inexpensive, and another bonus is that you don't have to cut up a whole chicken yourself if you are not very confident doing so.

44

These can be quite cost effective because you only need to remove and thaw just enough for what you need without any waste.

Outside of Christmas, turkey is largely overlooked. This is unfortunate as turkey is an economical way to feed a lot of people and there are so many ways you can use it.
As with chicken, you will get a better deal buying a whole turkey rather than just the breast. Turkey breast tends to be pretty expensive relatively, but other cuts like thighs can be much more reasonable. Look out for diced fresh turkey at the supermarket.

After Christmas you will find a lot of supermarkets will sell off their leftover stock of turkey, goose and duck, so if you can afford it, buy up a few and freeze for later use.

Turkey has the reputation of being a bit dry, and I have to say that using the darker meat from the thighs can result in quite chewy pieces rather than when you use the tender breast meat. But there is a solution for this – slow cooking!

Read on for reasons why you should invest in a slow cooker if you want to be a frugal Paleo cook.

Super Frugal Slow Cooker Savvy

If you want to save time and money, then look no further than the slow cooker. Load it up in the morning with your meat and vegetables, switch it on, and when you come home you are met with a delicious smell of dinner when you walk through the door.

Because slow cookers cook with a moist heat, the food you prepare in them become more savoury and tender than when you cook without one. This is especially useful for cooking cheaper cuts of meat that need slow cooking to make them meltingly juicy.

The types of meat ideally suited to slow cooking, whether using a slow cooker or your regular oven, are usually the cheaper cuts that when cooked normally would turn out quite tough, chewy or stringy.

Here are meats that work wonderfully in a slow cooker: Beef brisket, minced beef, heart, neck of lamb for casseroles, breast of lamb – boned and rolled, lamb mince for Shepherds Pie lamb shanks, lamb shoulder, pork shoulder, pork belly and turkey thigh pieces.

You can cook a whole chicken or a half leg of lamb in a slow cooker, as long as you have a large enough model.

Pig trotters are an acquired taste, but tasty they are! They cook well in a slow cooker, and the left over bones and gristle can be saved and used to make a stock. Ask your local butcher if they stock them.

Read on for some tasty slow cooker recipes using cheaper cuts of meat.

My beloved slow cooker that sits atop my kitchen work surface. Priceless!

Slow Cooker Beef Brisket

1.5kg/3lb 5oz beef brisket joint
Salt and black pepper
2 onions, thinly sliced
3 fresh bay leaves
350ml/12fl oz gluten free beer

Season the brisket joint generously with salt and black pepper.
Sprinkle the sliced onions and bay leaves over the bottom of the slow cooker, sit the brisket on top of the onions and pour over the beer.
Cook on low for 8-10 hours.

Slow Cooker Spicy Pork Belly

1 pork belly joint
1 tablespoon dried thyme
1 teaspoon salt
1 teaspoon ground fennel
1 teaspoon ground coriander
2 tablespoons olive oil

Crush thyme, salt, fennel and coriander together in a pestle and mortar and mix with the olive oil to make a thick paste. If the skin is not scored already, score the skin with a Stanley knife right into the fat layer, and rub in the paste. Make sure it is rubbed in deep into the scores. Leave the belly to marinate in the fridge for at least an hour, or overnight if you can wait that long.

Place the seasoned pork belly into the slow cooker, skin side up, add a glass of cider, or unsweetened apple juice, and cook on low for 7-8 hours.

Deli Style Herb Roast Chicken

3 – 4lb whole chicken, giblets removed
1 ½ litre cold water
1 teaspoon black pepper
2 teaspoons dried thyme
2 teaspoons dried rosemary
2 teaspoons dried oregano
2 tablespoons olive oil

In a very large bowl, mix together the water, salt, ½ tsp black pepper, 1tsp thyme, 1tsp rosemary, and 1 tsp of oregano. Sit the chicken in the liquid, and cover the bowl with cling film. Leave to marinate in the fridge overnight.

Rub the insides of the slow cooker pot with some olive oil, drain the chicken and place in the pot. Rub the chicken all over with the 2 tablespoons of olive oil, coating well, then sprinkle over the remaining thyme, black pepper, rosemary, and oregano, rub the spices over the skin. Turn the chicken breast side down in the slow cooker. Put the lid on and cook on high for one hour, then turn down to low and cook for a further 6 to 7 hours. Ensure the chicken is cooked right through. If there are any traces of blood or pink juices, then cook for another hour. Switch off the slow cooker and leave the chicken to rest in the pot for 15 minutes before serving.

The leftover cold chicken meat makes a
wonderful salad.

Roasted Lemon Chicken

3 – 4lb whole chicken
2 lemons
2 tablespoons olive oil
¼ teaspoon salt
½ teaspoon ground black pepper

Grease the inside of the slow cooker pot with a little olive oil. Remove any giblets from inside the chicken, and rub the whole chicken with olive oil. Season the skin with salt and black pepper.

Take the lemons and using a small sharp knife, pierce through the lemon skin and into the flesh a few times, then slice each lemon into three thick slices.

Push the lemon slices inside the chicken cavity, and lay the chicken breast side down in the slow cooker. Put the lid on and cook on low for 7 hours. Check for doneness before removing the chicken from the slow cooker. Remove the lemon slices and serve.

The chicken will have given off some juices in the pot while cooking, and this will be flavoured with the lemons, so once you have sliced the chicken ready to serve you could spoon over some of the lemony liquid for a bit of extra lemon zing.

Slow Roast Chilli Pork

3 lb pork shoulder joint
1 or 2 chilli's (depending on how hot you like it)
2 teaspoons chilli powder
1 clove of garlic, crushed
1 teaspoon ground black pepper
2 teaspoons dried oregano
1 teaspoon ground cumin
2 tablespoons olive oil

In a small bowl, mix together all the spice
ingredients with the olive oil. Rub the spice
mixture all over the pork joint until well coated.
Put the joint into the slow cooker, cover and cook
on high for one hour, then turn down to low for at
least 7 to 8 hours, or longer if needed. Check for
doneness before removing from the slow cooker.
Cover the joint with tin foil and leave to stand on
a warm plate for 10 – 15 minutes before slicing.

Roast Turkey Crown Roll

4 – 6lb turkey crown
375ml gluten free chicken stock
A little olive oil
1 onion, sliced
2 whole cloves of garlic
½ teaspoon paprika
½ teaspoon salt
½ teaspoon ground black pepper

Lay the sliced onion in the bottom of the slow
cooker pot, and push in the garlic cloves. Pour in
the chicken stock. Mix the dry spices and
seasoning together. Rub the turkey crown all over
with a little olive oil, and rub in the dry spice
mixture.
Sit the turkey crown in the pot with the onions
and stock. Cook on low for 8 hours and check for
doneness.
Remove the crown from the slow cooker and
leave to rest under some foil for 5 to 10 minutes.
Slice and serve with fresh vegetables.
You can use the pot juices spooned over the meat
and vegetables if you like.

Beef And Vegetable Stew

This recipe would benefit from searing the meat
and starting the vegetables off before adding to
the slow cooker, but if you are pressed for time
you can just throw everything into the pot
without preparation.

900g beef stewing steak
2 tablespoons olive oil
2 onions, chopped
2 teaspoons minced garlic, or 2 cloves, crushed
2 large carrots, peeled and sliced into coins
3 stalks of celery, diced
1 teaspoon salt
½ teaspoon black pepper
230g mushrooms, sliced
1 400g tin tomatoes
200ml gluten free beef stock
2 teaspoons Worcestershire Sauce
2 teaspoons thyme
1 bay leaf

In a frying pan, sear the beef stewing steak and
garlic in a little hot olive oil and tip into the slow
cooker. Add the vegetables to the frying pan with
the salt and pepper and cook for about 4 minutes
to soften. Add the vegetables to the slow cooker.
In a jug mix together the tinned tomatoes, beef
stock, Worcestershire Sauce, thyme and bay leaf,
and pour into the slow cooker over the meat and

vegetables. Sprinkle over the sliced mushrooms, mix everything well. Put on the lid and cook on medium for 7 hours. Stir well and remove the bay leaf before serving.

Recipes Using Cheaper Cuts Of Pork

We want to have maximum value for our pound, so seek out cheaper cuts of pork and use these recipes to turn them into tasty, nutritious meals that stretch that little bit further.

Look out for bacon on sale as buy one get one free, supermarket meat deals offering 3 different meats for £10, usually pork loin or shoulder steaks, diced pork, and bacon packs. Also look out for pork belly in shops and supermarket's as these are usually much cheaper than prime cuts of pork.

Pork shoulder joints are good value, and can provide you with a lot of meals such as slow roast pork, cold cuts and stir fry dishes.

Pork Belly With Sage And Apple

1.5kg/3lb 5oz pork belly, skin scored. Or score
the skin yourself with a Stanley knife
2 tbsp finely chopped fresh thyme leaves
1 tsp ground black pepper
2 tsp salt
3 medium apples, peeled, quartered, cored and
cut into thick slices
2 onions, sliced
A large handful of fresh sage leaves
200ml/7fl oz cider or unsweetened apple juice

Preheat the oven to 240C/475FGas 9.
Mix the thyme, salt and black pepper together in
a bowl. Rub this mixture all over the pork.
Place the pork in a baking dish and roast for 25-
30 minutes, or until the skin goes crisp. Reduce
the oven to 180C/350F/Gas 4 and roast for
another hour.
Mix the sliced apples with the onions, sage and a
little black pepper and arrange in the middle of a
small roasting tin.
Remove the pork from the oven, take it out of the
dish and place it on top of the apples and onions.
Return the pork to the oven and cook for a further
hour, or until the meat is really tender.
Pour any fat and juices from the first roasting
dish into a small saucepan. Stir in the cider or
apple juice, heat on high and bring to a simmer.
Cook for 3-4 minutes, stirring constantly. Strain

the juice through a sieve into a small saucepan and season with salt and pepper.
Transfer the cooked pork to a carving board. Scoop the apple and onion into a warmed serving bowl. Reheat the cider or apple juice sauce until bubbling, then stir it into the cooked apple and onions. Serve the pork and crackling cut into slices with the apple and sage sauce.

Pork Belly In Curry Sauce

Pork belly strips are often on sale in supermarkets, and I find these are easy to snip into even shaped bite-sized cubes with a pair of scissors.

900g pack of pork belly strips cut into cubes
25g lard
1 large onion, chopped
1 large eating apple, cored and sliced
1 heaped tablespoon curry powder
1 teaspoon minced garlic
½ teaspoon black pepper
1 tablespoon seedless raisins
400ml gluten free pork or chicken stock

Melt the lard in a thick-bottomed saucepan and fry the pork belly cubes lightly all over. Remove and set aside.
Fry the onion in the same saucepan until transparent but not browned.
Add the apple to the onions and cook until soft.
Stir in the curry powder and continue to fry the apples and onions for another 3 to 4 minutes.
Add the stock slowly stirring until well combined.
Add the minced garlic, black pepper, raisins and pork cubes back to the saucepan and stir well.
Bring to the boil, then turn down the heat to a slow simmer, put the saucepan lid on and cook

slowly for about 1 ½ hours until the meat is tender and meltingly soft.

Bacon With Red Cabbage

170g streaky bacon rashers
25g lard
227g onions, chopped
454g red cabbage, shredded
227g cooking apples, peeled, cored and sliced
1 bay leaf
1 teaspoon of honey
A pinch of black pepper
142ml water
1 teaspoon chopped parsley

Melt the lard in a heavy bottomed saucepan, and fry the onions until soft. Add the shredded cabbage to the pan of onions, along with the apples, water, bay leaf, honey and pepper. Mix everything well. Put on the saucepan lid and simmer the mixture for ½ hour, stirring occasionally. If the mixture starts to boil dry, add a little more water to keep everything moist. Snip the bacon rashers into bite size pieces. Sprinkle the bacon pieces over the top of the cabbage mixture, replace the lid and cook for another 15 minutes.
Serve on warmed plates sprinkled with the fresh chopped parsley.

Curried Pork Burgers

For the curry sauce:
1 tbsp olive oil
½ red onion, finely chopped
1 clove garlic, finely crushed
½ tsp ground cumin
½ tsp ground coriander
1 tbsp tomato puree
1½ tsp curry powder
200ml/7fl oz coconut milk

For the pork burgers:
110g/4oz pork mince
Salt and black pepper
1 tbsp olive oil

In deep frying pan, heat the olive oil, add the red
onion and garlic puree and cook for 2-3 minutes
over a medium heat.
Add the spices and tomato puree and stir well.
Gradually pour in the coconut milk, stirring after
each addition. Simmer the mixture for 5 minutes.
Season the pork mince with salt and pepper, and
form small burger shapes out of the mince. Heat
the olive oil in a frying pan and fry the burgers
for 2-3 minutes on each side until golden and
cooked all the way through. Pour the curry over
the burgers to serve.

Crispy Pork Salad

2 tbsp olive oil
70g/3oz pork mince
1 tsp ground cumin
½ tsp chilli flakes
The juice of 2 limes
Pinch of salt
2 tbsp chopped coriander or parsley
½ small Romaine lettuce, chopped
1 eating apple, cored and chopped

Heat the oil in a pan until very hot and add the pork mince, along with the spices and lime juice, and fry for 8 - 10 minutes until the mince has turned golden and crispy.
Stir through the coriander or parsley and take off the heat.
For the salad, mix together the Romaine lettuce and chopped apple.
To serve, place the salad on a plate and sprinkle over the pork.
Drizzle over a little olive oil if you wish.

Pan Fried Pork

Serves 2
2 x 75g/2 ½ oz pork steaks
2 tbsp olive oil
Salt and black pepper
3 tablespoons honey
2 pinch chilli flakes
150ml/5fl oz water
Bagged watercress salad

Put the honey, chilli flakes and water into a small frying pan and cook slowly for 5-6 minutes until reduced and thickened slightly. Leave to cool.
Put each pork steak between 2 sheets of cling film onto a chopping board. Using a rolling pin, bash and flatten the pork steaks to thin then out to about 5cm thickness all over. Brush the pork steaks with olive oil, sprinkle with salt and black pepper and sear in a hot frying pan in a little oil for two minutes on each side until cooked all the way through.
Remove from the heat and leave to rest for two minutes on a warm plate. Slice the pork into thick pieces and arrange on a bed of watercress.
Drizzle with the cooled dressing.

Pork Stir Fry

Serves 2
300g pork fillet, sliced
2 pinches chilli flakes
Olive oil
Salt and black pepper
3 garlic cloves, chopped
1 small onion, finely sliced
2 carrots, peeled and sliced into ribbons
4 small leeks, very finely sliced

Place the pork into a bowl with the chilli flakes, a teaspoon of olive oil, salt and black pepper and the garlic. Stir and leave to marinate for ten minutes.
Slice the carrots into long ribbons using a vegetable peeler.
Heat a wok, add a little olive oil and stir fry the pork for 2-3 minutes, remove and keep warm.
Add a little more olive oil to the wok. Add the onion, carrot and leeks and stir-fry for three minutes. Return the pork to the wok and stir well. Serve hot.

Bacon And Spinach Salad

Serves 2
100g/4oz spinach
100g/4oz pecans or walnuts, chopped
¼ onion, finely chopped
4 tbsp olive oil
½ tsp Dijon mustard
Salt and black pepper
4 tsp lemon juice
4 slices streaky bacon, grilled until crisp

Place the spinach into a salad bowl and sprinkle
with the pecans or walnuts. In a small mixing jug,
combine the olive oil, lemon juice, mustard, and
salt and pepper – beat together well with a fork or
small whisk.
Top the salad with the bacon, and drizzle over the
dressing. Serve right away.

Bacon And Vegetable Kebabs

Serves 2
12 cherry tomatoes
2 tbsp olive oil
12 rashers smoked streaky bacon
1 small courgette cut into thick slices
12 whole button mushrooms, or 6 larger
mushrooms cut in half
Salt and black pepper

Preheat the oven to 200C/400F/Gas 6.
Soak four wooden skewers in water for 15
minutes to prevent them from burning.
Roll the bacon rashers up into individual rolls.
Thread the bacon, mushrooms, tomatoes and
courgette chunks alternately onto the wooden
skewers. Rub the olive oil over the kebabs, and
season with salt and black pepper.
Heat a griddle pan or frying pan until smoking,
then add the kebabs and char grill for two
minutes on each side, or until the bacon has
begun to brown.
Put the kebabs onto a baking tray and cook in the
oven for five minutes, or until the bacon is
completely cooked through.

Bacon And Cabbage Soup

Serves 2
2 tbsp olive oil
2 clove garlic, crushed
2 leeks, finely chopped
6 rashers bacon, finely chopped
1 Savoy cabbage, shredded
1 ltr/2 pints gluten free chicken stock
2 tbsp fresh parsley, finely chopped

Salt and black pepper

Heat the olive oil in a saucepan over a medium heat. Add the crushed garlic and chopped leeks and fry 2-3 minutes until soft.
Add the chopped bacon and continue to fry for another 3-4 minutes until the bacon starts to crisp and brown.
Add the shredded Savoy cabbage and fry, stirring regularly, for 2-3 minutes, until the cabbage is soft.
Add the stock and bring to the boil. Reduce the heat and simmer for 10 minutes.
Add the chopped parsley and stir well.
You can either blend the soup together with a hand-blender to make it completely smooth. Or if you prefer it to be chunky, blend half of the soup and mix it back in with the remaining unblended soup. Bring the soup back to the boil. Season with salt and pepper before serving.

Sausages Wrapped In Bacon

My all time favourite! I cook a tray of these up to
snack on when I'm feeling peckish.

5 chipolata sausages
5 rashers streaky bacon
1 tbsp olive oil
Salt and black pepper to taste

Preheat the oven to 200C/400F/Gas 6.
Lay the bacon out flat on a chopping board.
Sprinkle over the bacon with a little salt and
pepper.
Place one sausage at the end of each rasher of
bacon and roll the sausage up in the bacon.
Heat the oil in an ovenproof frying pan, add the
bacon-wrapped sausages and fry for a couple of
minutes until lightly browned all over.
Place the sausage and bacon rolls onto a baking
tray and cook in the oven until golden-brown and
completely cooked through.

Sausage Casserole

Look out for gluten-free sausages in your local supermarket. There are a number of companies that produce gluten-free sausages through the major supermarket chains, but most of the supermarkets also produce their own label gluten-free sausages that are usually much cheaper, but just as tasty!

This recipe serves 6, and any extra portions can be frozen down for use at a later date.

1–2 tbsp olive oil
12 good quality gluten free pork sausages
6 rashers rindless streaky bacon,
2 large onions, sliced
2 garlic cloves, crushed
½ tsp hot chilli powder
½ tsp paprika
1 x 400g can chopped tomatoes
300ml/10fl oz gluten free chicken stock
100ml water
2 tbsp tomato purée
1 tbsp Worcestershire sauce
1 tbsp runny honey
1 tsp dried mixed herbs
2 bay leaves
Salt and black pepper

Heat a tablespoon of the olive oil in a large frying pan and fry the sausages gently for 10 minutes, turning regularly until browned all over. Remove and keep warm in a large casserole dish.

Snip the bacon rashers into pieces and cook in the frying pan until they begin to brown and crisp then add to the sausages in the casserole dish.

Place the sliced onions in the frying pan and fry until they start to soften, stirring often.

Add the garlic and cook for 2–3 minutes.

Sprinkle over the chilli powder and paprika and cook together for a few seconds.

Stir in the tomatoes, chicken stock, tomato purée, Worcestershire sauce, honey and herbs. Pour in the water and bring to the boil.

Put the sausages and bacon back into the frying pan with the sauce, return to a simmer, then reduce the heat, cover the pan loosely with foil or a lid and leave to simmer very gently for 30 minutes, stirring from time to time. Check to see if the liquid is boiling away, and add a little more water if necessary.

Season to taste with salt black pepper and serve.

Live Well On Liver

If you are looking for an inexpensive source of high-quality meat, look no further than liver!

Liver was a staple food amongst our grandparent's generation but seems to have fallen out of favour with younger generations.

This is a shame because nutritionally liver is packed full of high quality protein, and all the amino acids essential for human life.

Liver is also a fantastic source of vitamin A, vitamin D, all the B vitamins, vitamin C, and iron.

Calves' liver and chicken livers are most commonly used in the UK. Lamb's livers are slightly stronger than those from calves but taste equally good.

Pigs' liver is much stronger in taste than lambs' liver, and often turns out much tougher after cooking too. Liver is classically served with crisp bacon, and fried onions.

The cheapest liver to buy is usually pigs' liver, unless you see some in the reduced section.

Liver needs to be very fresh. Look for firm, glistening livers with a deep pink-red colour. If the liver looks pale and insipid, pass it over for something else.

Liver is best used on the day of purchase, but it will keep it in the fridge for 1-2 days.

Sliced thinly and quickly grilled or fried and served pink, liver is tender and full of flavour.

Chicken livers can be pan-fried whole and served pink.

Ox liver is the toughest and strongest tasting liver and needs slow cooking, so braise or stew for best results with lots of onions and tomatoes.

You can buy liver fresh from your local butchers shop, and they often sell it off at reduced prices at the end of the day, so if you can time your visit for just before closing time you may be in for a nutritious bargain!

Supermarkets usually sell liver in sealed packs both fresh and frozen. Although frozen livers are usually cheaper than fresh livers to buy, I have never been disappointed with the quality of frozen liver, so buy whichever is more convenient for you.

Lush liver before the magic happens!

Traditional Liver And Bacon Made Paleo

Serves 4
900g liver
900g streaky bacon rashers
Pepper and salt, to taste
A small piece of lard
2 tbsp lemon-juice
150ml water

Slice the liver into thin pieces. Snip the bacon rashers into bite size pieces with a pair of kitchen scissors.
Melt the lard in a frying pan and fry the bacon first. Once the bacon is crisp remove the pieces from the pan leaving behind as much bacon fat as possible and keep warm.
Season the liver slices with a little salt and pepper, then fry the liver pieces in the bacon fat and lard in the frying pan. Turn the liver occasionally to prevent burning, and when done remove from the pan and add to the crispy bacon.
Add the lemon-juice and water to the frying pan and bring to the boil stirring together all the pan juices, simmer for one minute, then pour the pan juices over the liver and bacon to serve.

Liver And Bacon With Onions And Gravy

Serves 4
450g/1lb lambs' liver
25g/1oz lard
2 tbsp olive oil
1 onion, halved lengthways and sliced
125g/4½oz streaky bacon rashers, cut into 4 pieces
1 gluten free beef stock cube
500ml/18fl oz boiling water
2 tsp tomato puree
1 tsp runny honey
Salt and black pepper

Rinse and dry the liver on kitchen paper. Melt the lard with the olive oil in a large frying pan over a high heat.
Season the liver with salt and pepper, then fry each slice in the hot fat for 1–2 minutes on each side until lightly browned. Remove the liver slices and keep warm.
Reduce the heat and add the sliced onion and cook for a minute or two until softened.
Add the bacon to the pan and fry, stirring often, for 10 minutes or until the onion is pale golden-brown and the bacon is beginning to crisp.
Dissolve the stock cube, honey and tomato puree in the boiled water and pour slowly into the pan, stirring as you go.

Bring the pan to a simmer and cook over a medium heat until everything is cooked through. Season with salt and black pepper.
Return the liver to the pan with the onion gravy for 2 minutes to warm it through and finish cooking the liver.
Serve the liver and bacon with some cooked sliced carrots and Brussels sprouts, or cabbage.

Liver Wrapped In Bacon

Serves 2
170g/6oz lambs' liver, cut into six strips
6 rashers streaky bacon
2 tbsp olive oil
Salt and black pepper

Lay the bacon rashers onto a chopping board and sprinkle with salt and pepper. Place one strip of the liver at one end of each bacon rasher. Roll the liver up in the bacon to make a cigar shape and secure each roll with a cocktail stick.
Heat the olive oil in a frying pan and fry the liver and bacon rolls for 5-7 minutes, turning regularly to ensure they cook on all sides. Nice served hot with pan fried shredded cabbage.

Terrific Ways With Tinned Tuna

Tinned tuna is an essential store cupboard staple food that should be on every thrifty Paleo eaters shopping list.

Tinned tuna can be a good source of omega-3 fatty acids. It can sometimes contains over 300 milligrams per serving, so good for the heart as well as the pocket! It also contains good sources of Vitamin A, Choline, Vitamin D, Calcium, Iron, Magnesium, Phosphorus, Potassium, and Zinc.

You can often buy tinned tuna in multi-packs from supermarkets at a much cheaper price than when you buy individual tins.

Tuna comes packed in either brine, spring water or vegetable oil. As we want to avoid vegetable oils in our diet, then we should be buying tuna packed in either water or brine.

You will also notice that you can buy tuna steak, tuna chunks or tuna flakes, with the flaked tuna being the cheapest option. For quality reasons, the best sort to buy would be tuna steak when used in cooking. Tuna chunks are fine served as they are in cold salads, and even flaked tuna can be tasty and versatile when it is to be mashed and mixed with mayonnaise.

Tinned tuna – a staple ingredient of any Paleo cupboard, ethically caught of course!

Basic Tuna Mayo Salad

This is so versatile, and you can add different ingredients to the mix depending on what you have in the fridge.

Serves: 4
1 170g tin tuna, drained
1 small stick celery, chopped
2 tablespoons mayonnaise
1 pinch salt
4 sliced ripe tomatoes
1 cucumber, sliced
Mixed salad leaves of your choice

In a mixing bowl, mix together the drained tuna, celery, mayonnaise and salt until well combined. Spread salad leaves over cold plates, top with slices of tomato and cucumber, then spoon the tuna mayo mixture into the centre of each plate.

Family Tuna Dinner In Minutes

Serves: 6
1 tablespoon olive oil
1/2 green pepper, sliced
1 small onion, thinly sliced
1 clove garlic, crushed
1 teaspoon salt
2 teaspoons dried rosemary
120ml of tomato passata
3 tins tuna in water, drained

Heat the olive oil in a large frying pan over medium heat. Add the green pepper, onion and garlic and cook stirring until softened. Stir in the salt, rosemary and passata. Bring to the boil and simmer, stirring constantly for 5 minutes. Mix in the tuna, and cook for 5 more minutes to blend the flavours before serving.

Tuna and Orange Salad

Serves 2
1 (185g) tin tuna in springwater, drained
1 orange - peeled, sectioned and cut into pieces
1 1/2 tablespoons mayonnaise
2 tablespoons cashew halves
1 teaspoon ground ginger
1 teaspoon lemon juice
salt and freshly ground black pepper to taste
handful fresh spinach

In a medium bowl combine the tuna, orange
pieces, mayonnaise, cashews, ginger, lemon
juice, salt and pepper. Mix well. Serve over a bed
of spinach or lettuce leaves.

Tuna With Peppers And Mushrooms

Serves: 4
2 tbsp olive oil
1 large onion, chopped
250g fresh mushrooms, quartered
1 tbsp wholegrain mustard
Zest of 1 lemon
4 tbsp lemon juice
1 garlic clove, crushed
280g jar of roasted red peppers
185g tin tuna, drained
Salt and black pepper

Heat the olive oil in a frying pan and add the onion. Cook for 5 minutes or until softened but do not brown. Add the mushrooms, season with salt and pepper and cook, stirring occasionally, until the mushrooms soften.
Stir in the mustard, lemon zest and juice, and garlic clove. Cook for a couple more minutes. Drain and slice the jar of red peppers, then add to the pan.
Tip in the drained tuna and stir well to combine. Heat through for another minute then serve with a crunch salad on the side.

Tuna And Tomato Omelette

Serves: 4
6 eggs
8 fresh tomatoes
10 fresh basil leaves
1 tbsp olive oil
185g tin tuna, drained
5 tbsp mayonnaise
Salt and black pepper

Beat the eggs with a little salt and black pepper. Chop the tomatoes and mix with the eggs. Chop the basil leaves and add to the egg and tomato mixture.
Preheat the grill to high. Heat the olive oil in a large frying pan and pour in the egg and tomato mixture, spreading the ingredients out evenly over the base of the pan. Cook over a medium heat, for a minute then turn down the heat if the omelette starts to brown too quickly. When the omelette is almost set, put it under the grill to finish cooking the top.
Mix the drained tuna with the mayonnaise, and season with a little black pepper. Slice the omelette into 4 quarters and set each piece onto a warm plate. Spoon the tuna mixture onto each portion. Serve with some baby leaf spinach or salad leaves of your choice.

Go To Work On An Egg

Most of you reading this book will be too young to remember the TV advertisements of the 1950's featuring comedian Tony Hancock, where The British Egg Marketing Board pushed the slogan 'Go To Work On An Egg'. Our parents certainly would have known about the adverts as they became quite popular.

Although the old black & white adverts may not look as flash or polished as today's adverts, the messages conveyed in those adverts are still as relevant today.

Eggs are one of the most nutritious foods money can buy, and compared to the price of meat, eggs are a much cheaper way of getting high quality protein into your diet.

They are a natural source of many nutrients including vitamins and minerals in perfect balance.

They are rich in vitamin B2 (riboflavin), vitamin B12 and vitamin D. Eggs also contain vitamin A and a number of other B vitamins including folate, biotin, pantothenic acid and choline.

Eggs also contain essential minerals and trace elements, including phosphorus, iodine and selenium.

Eggs are also quick and easy to cook, so even if you are not the best cook in the world, with a little practice you could rustle up some tasty scrambled eggs, or an omelette without too much trouble.

Even easier to prepare are boiled eggs, so pop a couple of eggs into boiling water while you have your morning shower, and when you are done you will have breakfast ready and waiting for you!

Hard-boiled eggs are always handy to keep in the fridge. You can peel and eat one as a snack when you get peckish. Or make up a plate of devilled eggs for a more decadent snack, or to add to a healthy salad dish.

Don't keep eggs just for breakfast! Try some of these tasty egg recipes to follow.

Simple Herb Omelette

Simple, clean and fresh! Serve this as a light lunch, or chill it, cut into slices and mix with a crisp salad to take to work with you.

Serves 2
4 eggs
2 tbsp chopped fresh parsley
2 tbsp chopped fresh chives
Salt and black pepper
1 tbsp lard or olive oil for frying

In a large mixing bowl, beat the eggs and herbs together until the egg mixture is pale. Season with salt and black pepper to taste.
Heat the lard or olive oil in a frying pan over a medium heat, add the egg mixture and cook for 3 to 4 minutes, or until the eggs have set, and the omelette is starting to brown. Flip the omelette over to cook on the other side for just a minute. Slide onto a plate and cut in half. Divide between two plates and serve with some baby leaf spinach.

Egg And Corned Beef Hash

Serves: 4.
45ml/3tbsp olive oil
350g/12oz cauliflower, diced and steamed for 5 minutes
1 large onion, chopped
1 green pepper, deseeded and chopped
1 400g tin chopped tomatoes
1 340g tin corned beef, diced
1 pinch of dried chilli flakes
4 large eggs
Salt and black pepper

Heat a large non-stick frying pan, add the olive oil, cauliflower, onion and pepper and sauté over a medium heat for 6-8 minutes until soft and the onions start to brown.
Stir in the tomatoes and corned beef and cook for a further 2 minutes. Season with salt and black pepper.
Make four shallow hollows in the mixture and carefully crack an egg into each hollow. Cover the pan with a lid or a sheet of foil and cook over a medium heat for 7 or 8 minutes or until the eggs are set.

Tomato And Aubergine Baked Eggs

Serves 4
1 red pepper, deseeded and chopped
1 large onion, sliced
1 aubergine, chopped into bite size pieces
1 clove garlic, crushed
2 tbsp olive oil
1 400g tin chopped tomatoes
2 tbsp gluten free Pesto sauce from a jar
4 large eggs
1 tsp dried mixed herbs
Salt and black pepper

Preheat the oven to 200C/Fan 180C/400F/Gas
Mark6. Mix together the aubergine and peppers
and place in a baking dish. Add the onion, garlic,
olive oil and seasoning and stir everything
together to coat well. Bake for 20mins then
remove from the oven.
Stir in the tomatoes and pesto. Make four hollows
in the vegetable mixture, then crack an egg into
each hollow and cover the dish with foil. Bake
for 15-20 minutes until the eggs are set.

Warm Pepper Frittata

Serves 4
6 large eggs
2tbsp olive oil
1 large onion, chopped
3 peppers, deseeded and chopped
Any leftover cooked vegetables you may have
1 tsp curry powder
Salt and black pepper

Heat the olive oil in a large frying pan, add the onion and peppers, sauté over a medium heat for about 8 minutes until golden.
Add the curry powder and any leftover vegetables to the pan, stir everything well and cook for 1 minute.
Beat the eggs in a bowl with a little salt and pepper, and pour into the pan over the vegetables, stirring gently until the egg starts to set. Cover the pan with a lid or foil and cook for around 8 minutes or until the egg has almost set.
Slide the pan under a hot grill and cook until the top is golden. Serve cut into wedges with a green salad.

Frittata can be made with just about anything, and it is great hot or cold so you can pack up slices for lunch and take them to work with you.

Baked English Breakfast

This is great for a family Sunday breakfast. You can rustle this dish up while reading the papers, and there is no frying pan to watch!

Serves 4
8 large eggs
4 gluten free sausages
4 rashers bacon
2 large fresh tomatoes, halved
8 large mushrooms
Olive oil
Salt and black pepper

Preheat the oven to 200C Fan 180C Gas Mark 6. Grease a large baking dish with a little olive oil and place the sausages inside and bake for 10 minutes.
Turn the sausages over then add the bacon, tomato and mushrooms. Season well with a little salt and black pepper. Return to the over for another 10 minutes.
Remove the baking dish from the oven and move around the contents to make room for the eggs. Crack the eggs and add to the dish. Return the dish to the oven and cover the tops with lid or foil. Bake for 8 minutes until the eggs are cooked through.

Spinach Baked Eggs with Salsa

Serves 2
7g lard
4 large eggs
100g fresh spinach leaves
Nutmeg
2 large tomatoes, chopped
25g pitted black olives, chopped
2tsp extra virgin olive oil
1tbsp freshly chopped parsley
2 anchovies, drained, halved

Preheat the oven to 180C/Fan 160C/Gas Mark 4.
Melt the lard in the pan and sauté the spinach
until just wilted. Season with salt, pepper and a
little pinch of nutmeg.
Divide the spinach between two large ramekins.
Leave to cool for a minute then crack 2 eggs into
each ramekin.
Put the ramekins into a roasting dish and pour
enough boiling water to come halfway up the
sides of the dishes. Bake for 15min or until just
set.
Put the chopped tomatoes and olives in a bowl
and mix together with the olive oil and chopped
parsley.
When the eggs are cooked, divide the anchovy
among the ramekins, and top with the chopped
tomato salsa before serving.

Mushroom Omelette

This has to be one of my favourite omelette recipes. You can make omelettes with lots of different fillings, but I think mushrooms taste wonderful when combined with eggs.

Serves 2
50g/2oz lard or olive oil
200g/4oz mushrooms, sliced
4 eggs, beaten
Salt and black pepper
Topping:
3 tbsp olive oil
100g/1¾ mushrooms

In a large frying pan heat the lard or oil and add the mushrooms. Cook for three minutes until soft. Add the egg and season with salt and black pepper. Spread the mushrooms evenly in the egg around the pan. Cook on a low heat for 4-5 minutes until the egg is cooked.
Slide the omelette onto a warm plate and keep warm.
To make the topping, melt the oil in a small pan, add the mushrooms and fry for four minutes until soft and golden. Season with a little black pepper. Cut the omelette into two and divide between two warm plates. Spoon the fried mushrooms on top

of each omelette half, fold each half over to sandwich the mushroom filling and serve.

Eggs, Bacon And Butternut Squash

Serves 2
2 large eggs
2 thick slices of butternut squash with the skin on
2 tsp olive oil
4 rashers back bacon
50g/4oz mushrooms, sliced
2 spring onions, sliced
Salt and black pepper

Preheat the oven to 200C/Fan 180C/400F/Gas Mark 6. Place the butternut squash slices onto a baking sheet and brush a little olive oil over the top. Season with a little salt and black pepper. Bake for 20 minutes or until the flesh is soft. Heat the remaining oil in a frying pan, add the bacon and sauté until the bacon is crisp. Add the mushrooms and onion and sauté until soft. Spoon the bacon mixture on top of the butternut squash and make a hollow in the centre of the mixture. Crack an egg into the hollow of each squash and bake for about 10minutes until the egg is set. Serve hot.

###

Thank you for buying this book, and I hope you have found some tasty but frugal recipes in here that you can work into your weekly menu.

If you would like more Paleo/Caveman recipes then you may be interested in my book: Paleo/Caveman Diet and Gluten Free Recipes Tailored For British Tastes Using Foods Commonly Available In English Stores And Supermarkets

Printed in Great Britain
by Amazon.co.uk, Ltd.,
Marston Gate.